Mandala Art
— ADULT COLORiNG BOOK —

Copyright © 2020 Coloring Book Kim

Relaxing coloring book for adults with
hand drawn drawings mandalas,
covered with delicate ornaments.

ISBN: 9798677255182

For more informations and to stay updated
on new coloring books visit our web site at

www.coloringbookkim.com

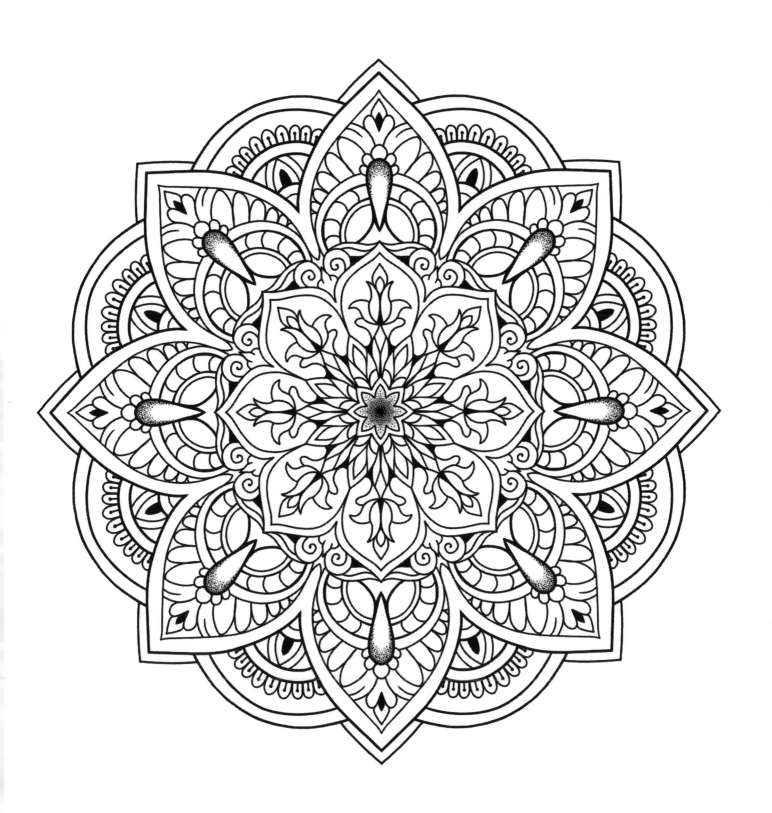

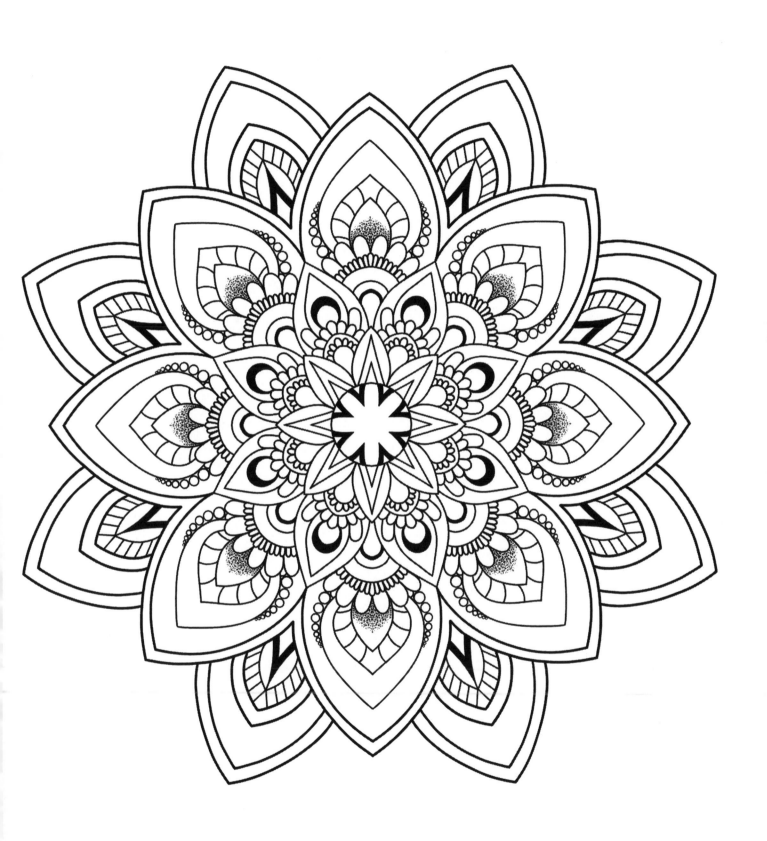

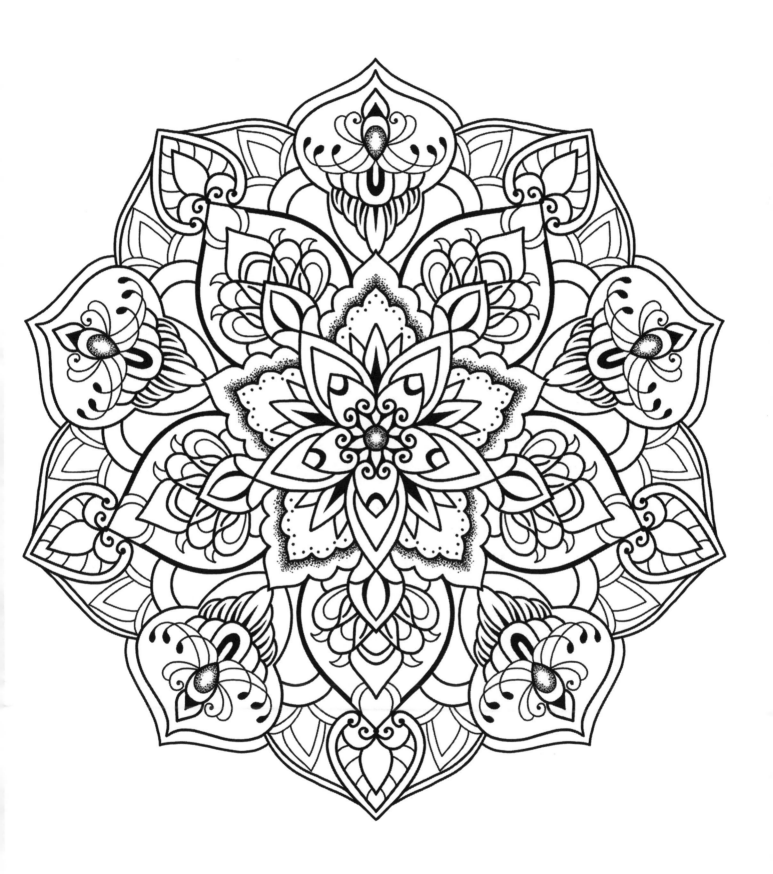

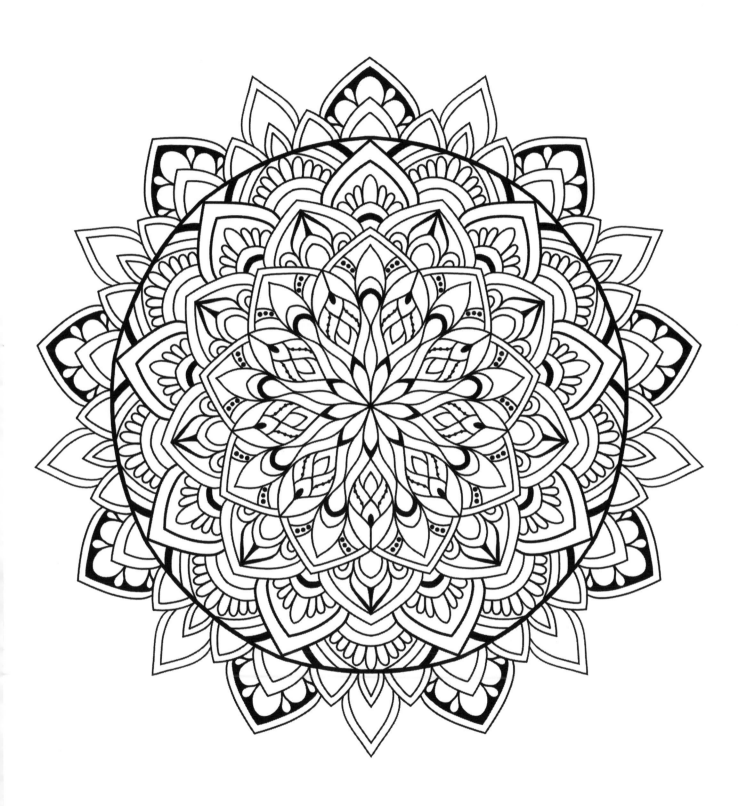

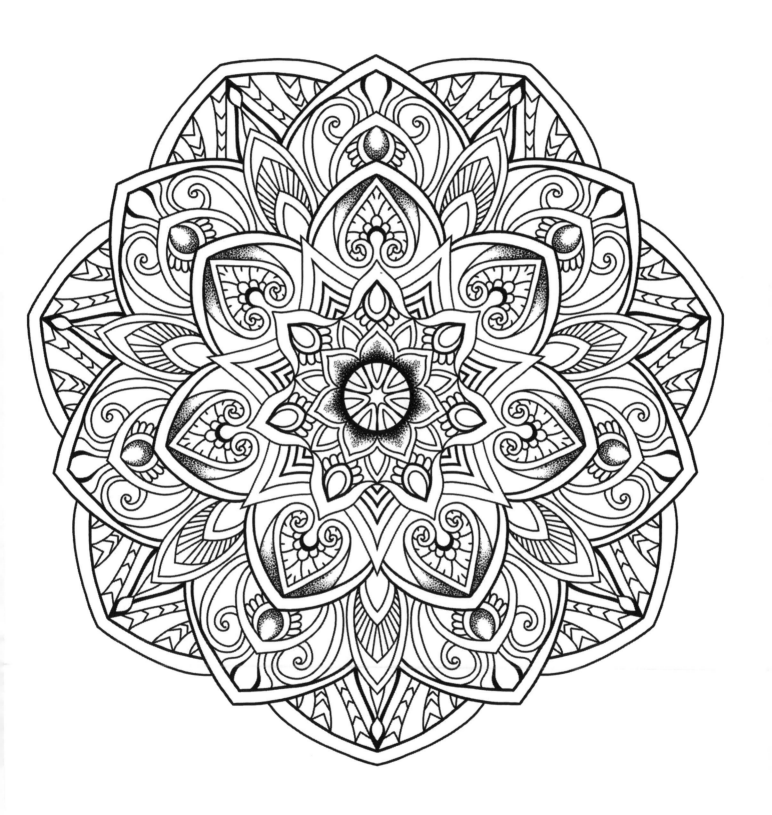

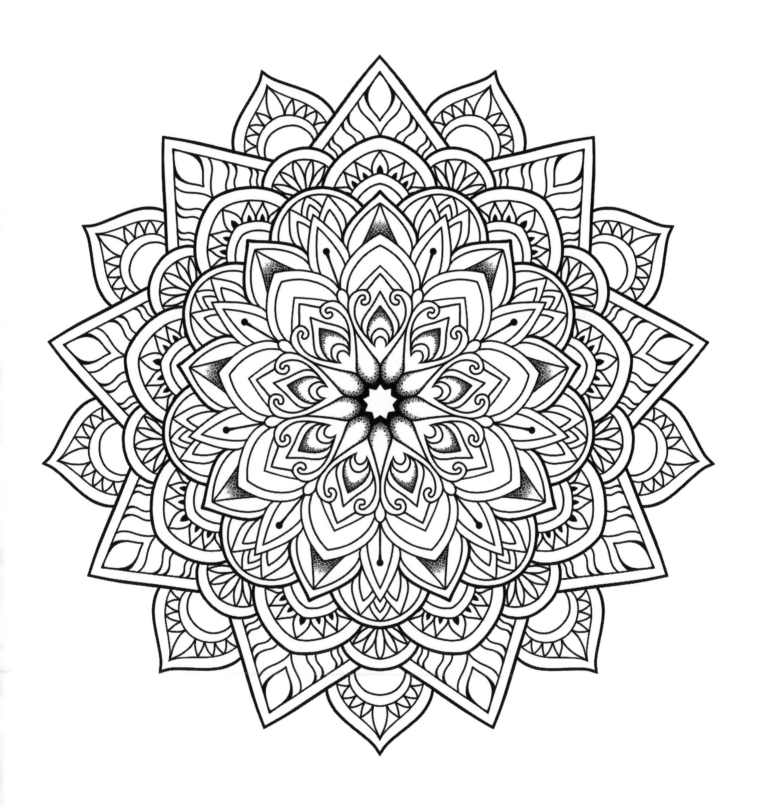

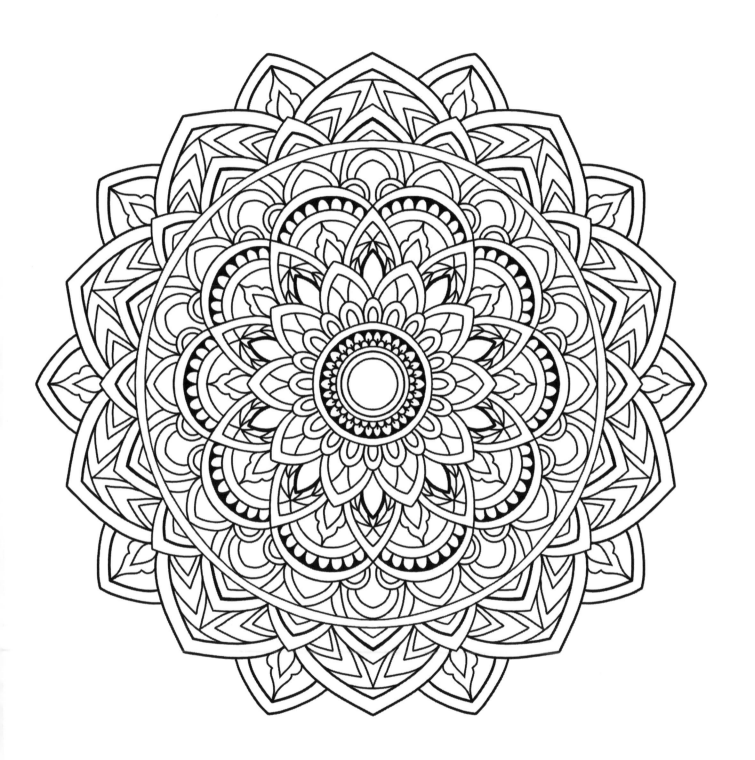

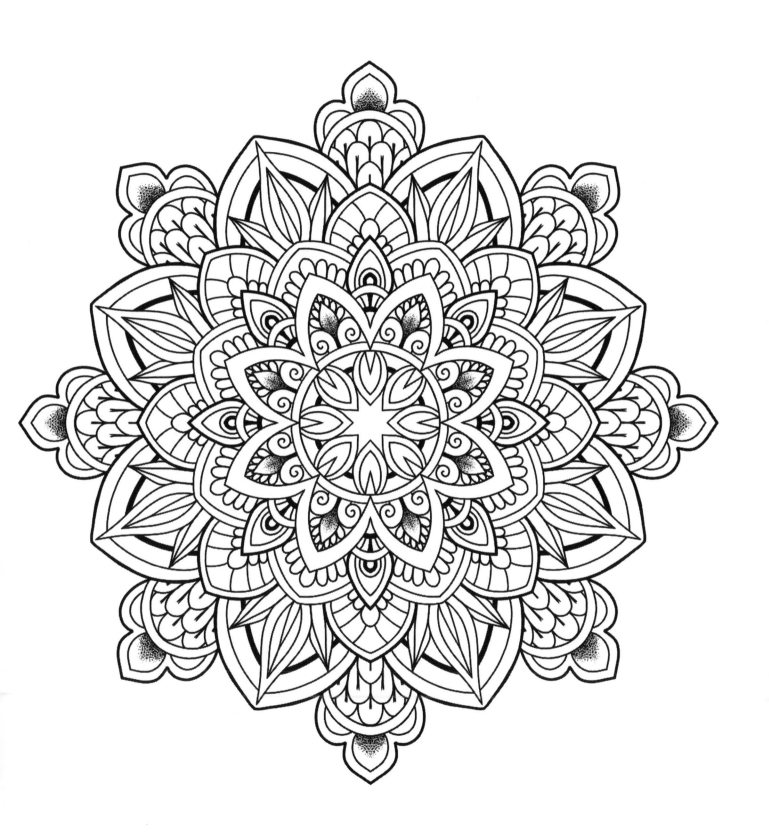

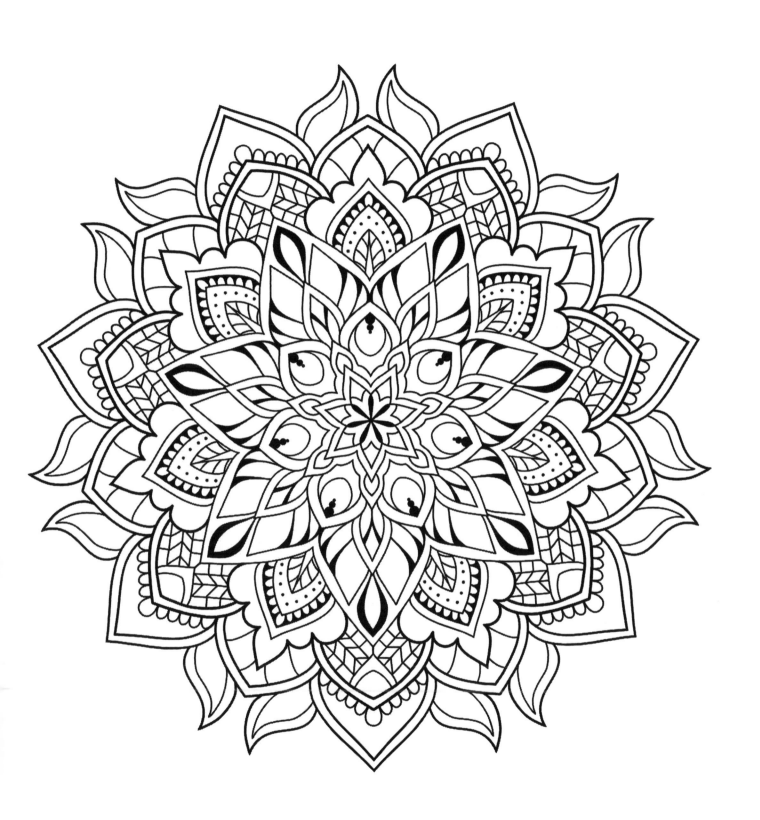

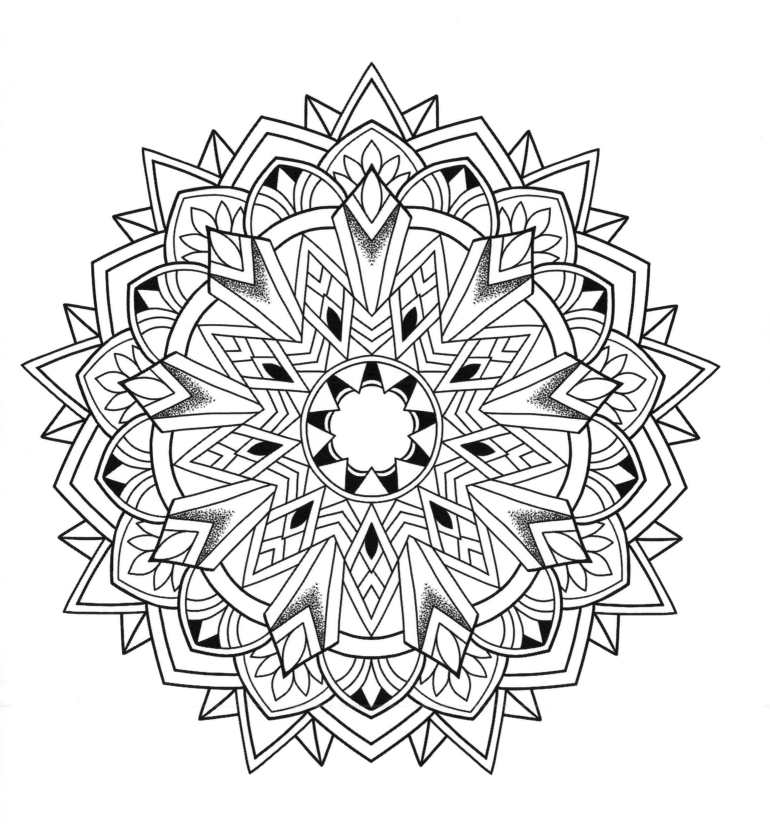

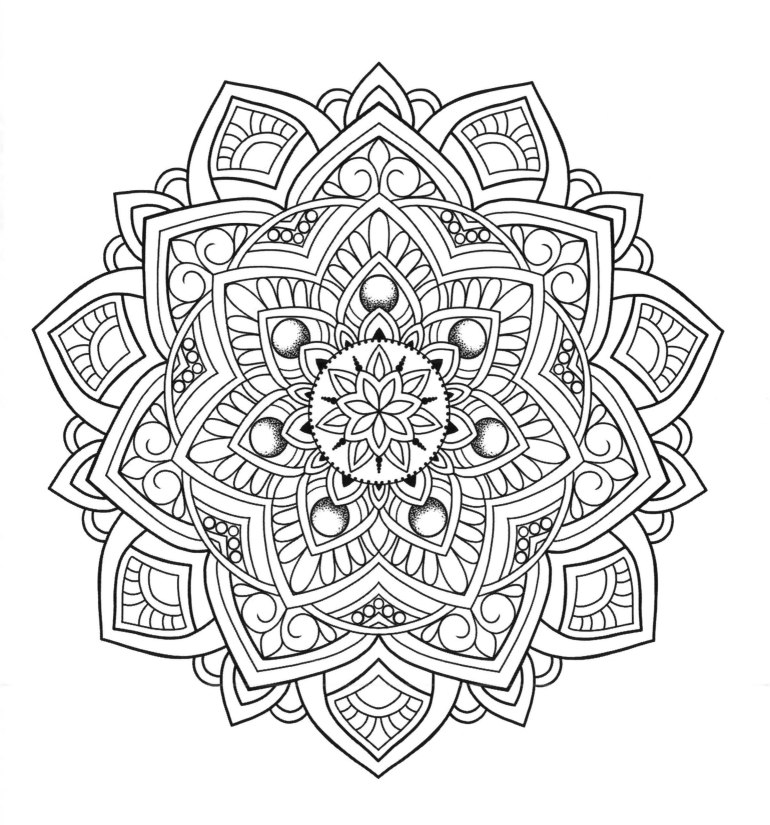

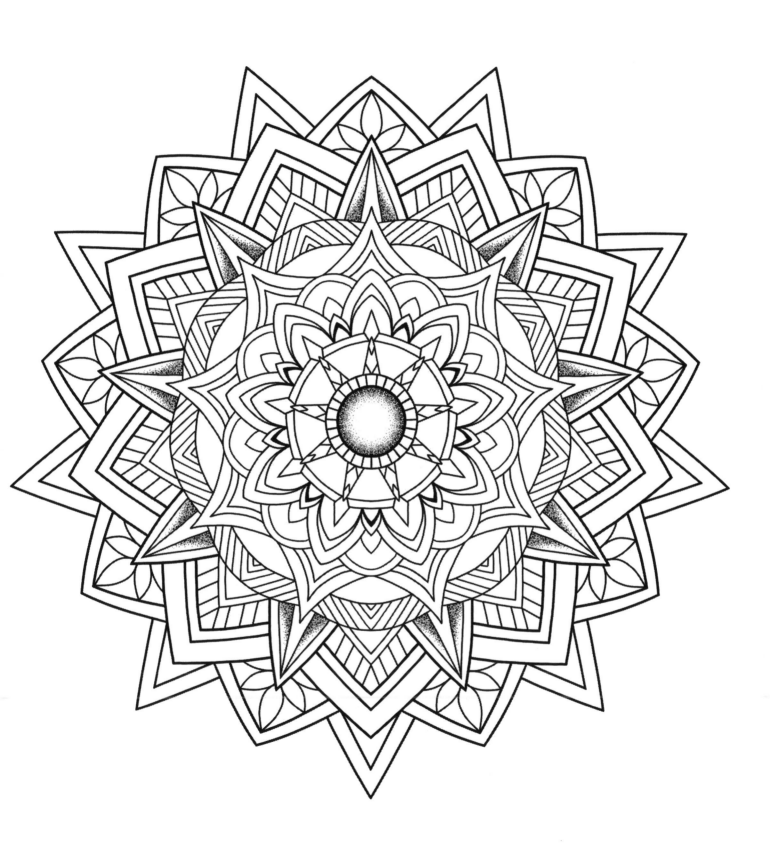

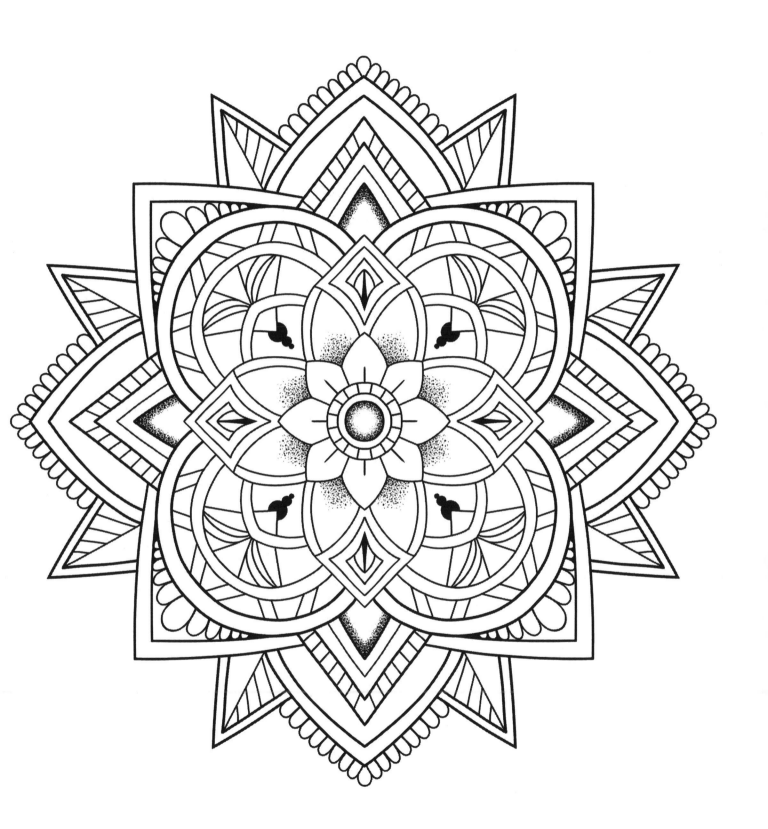

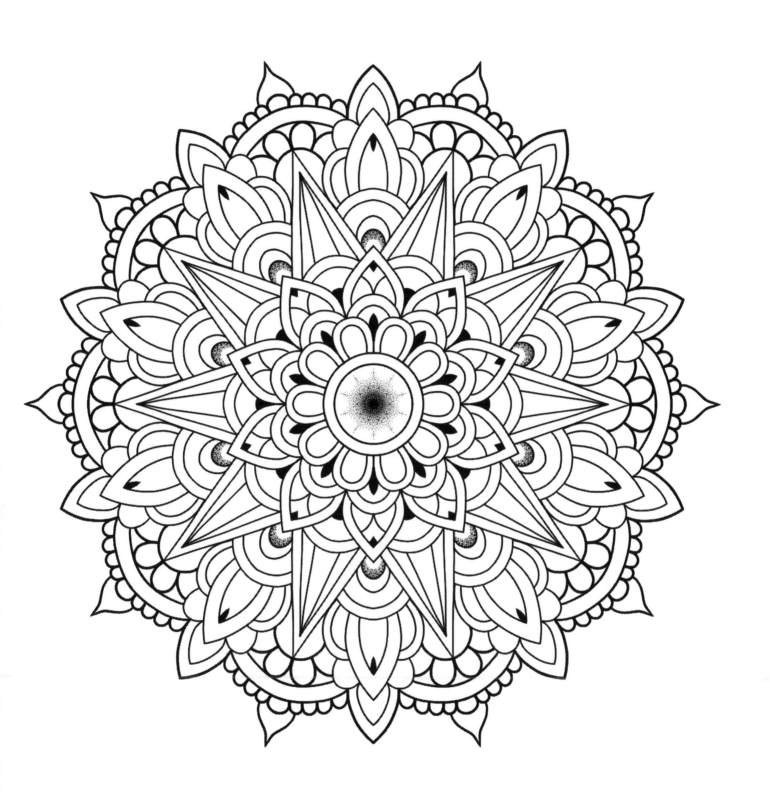

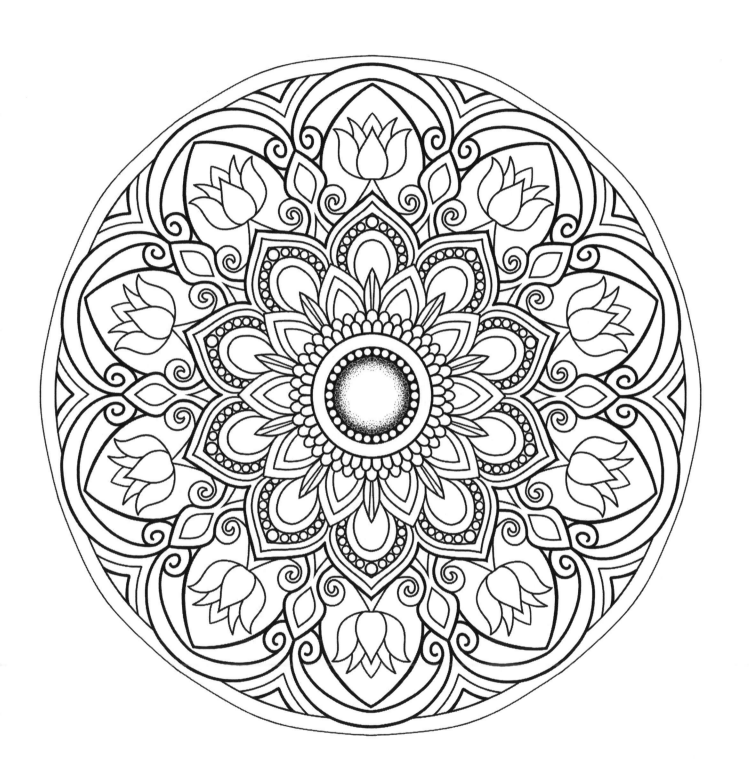

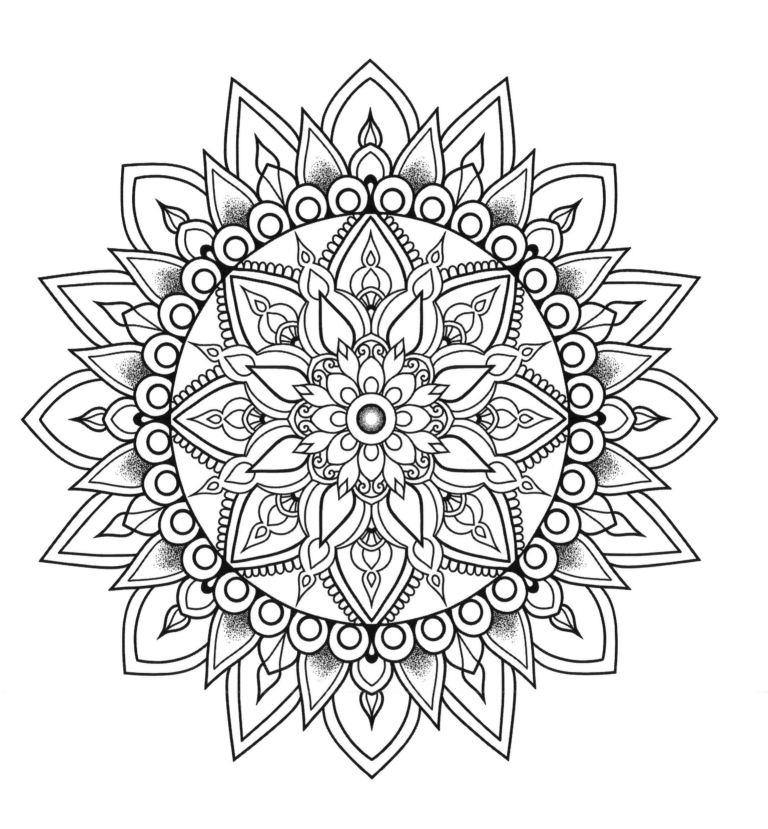

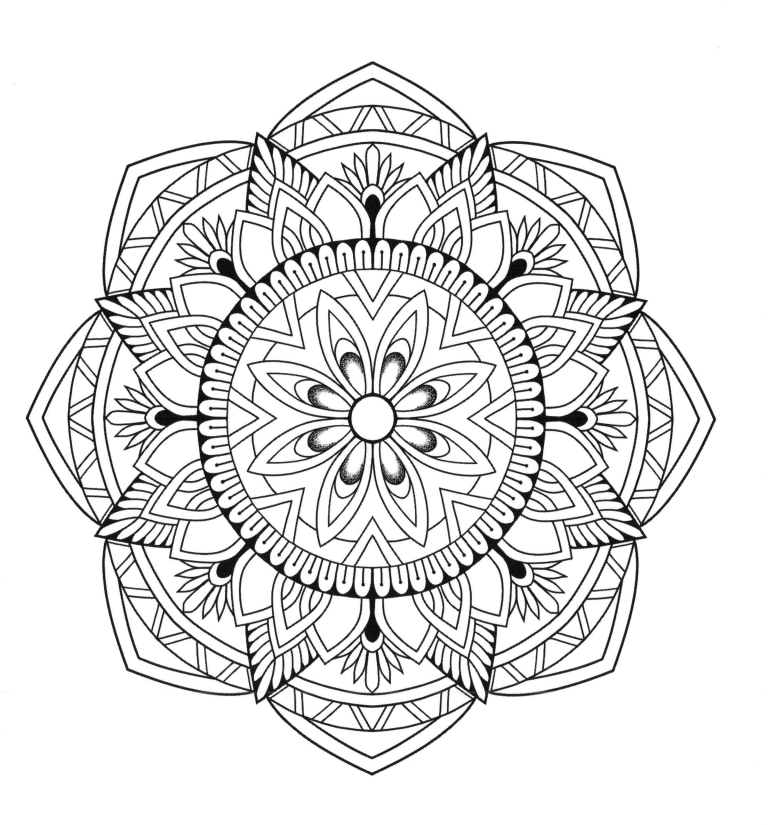

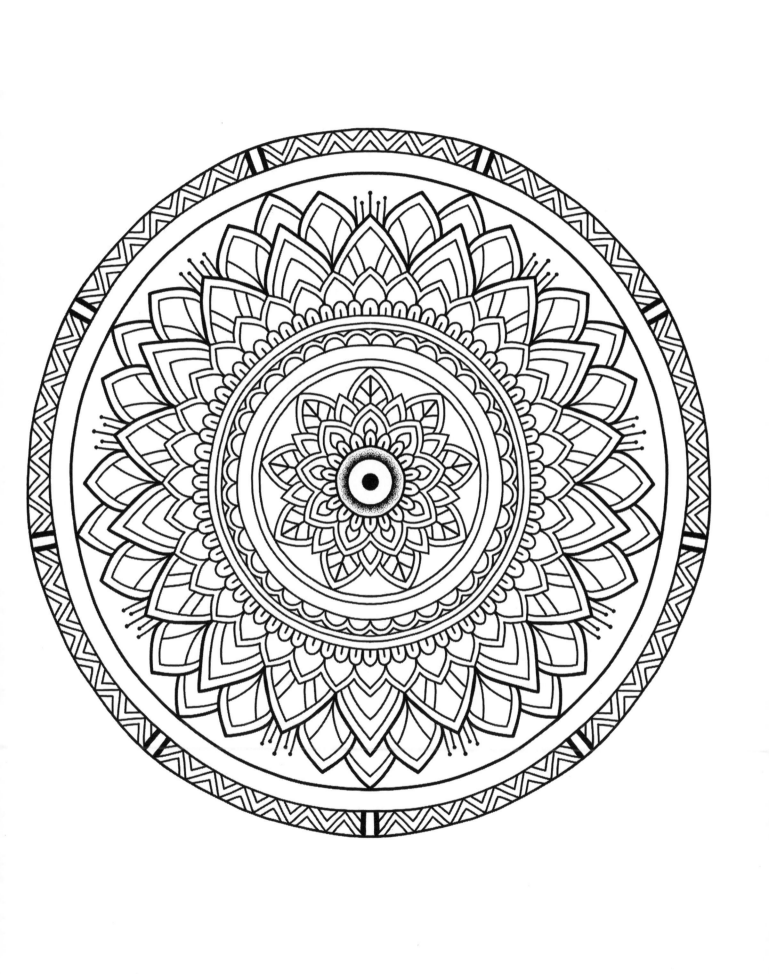

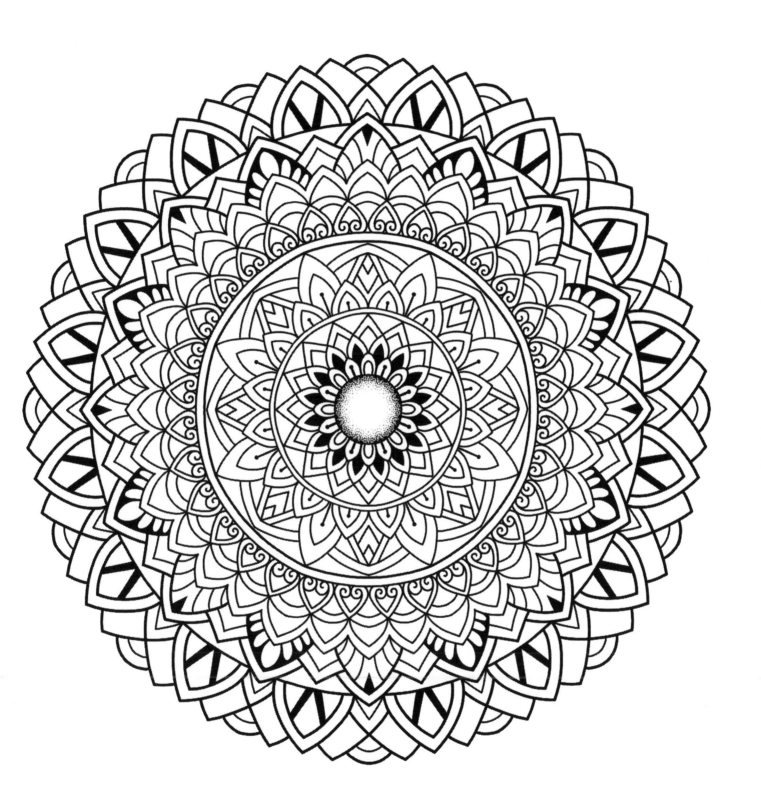

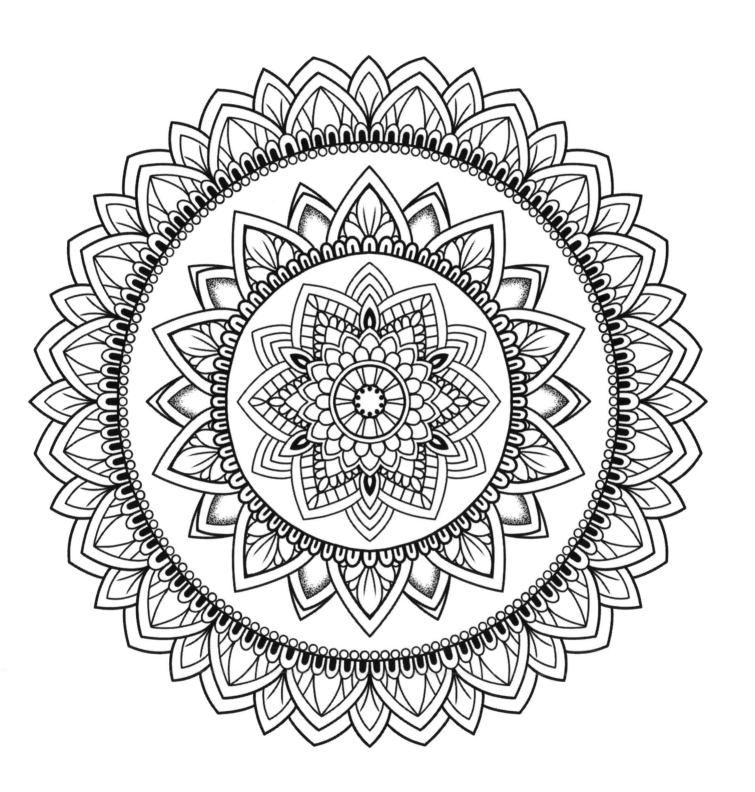

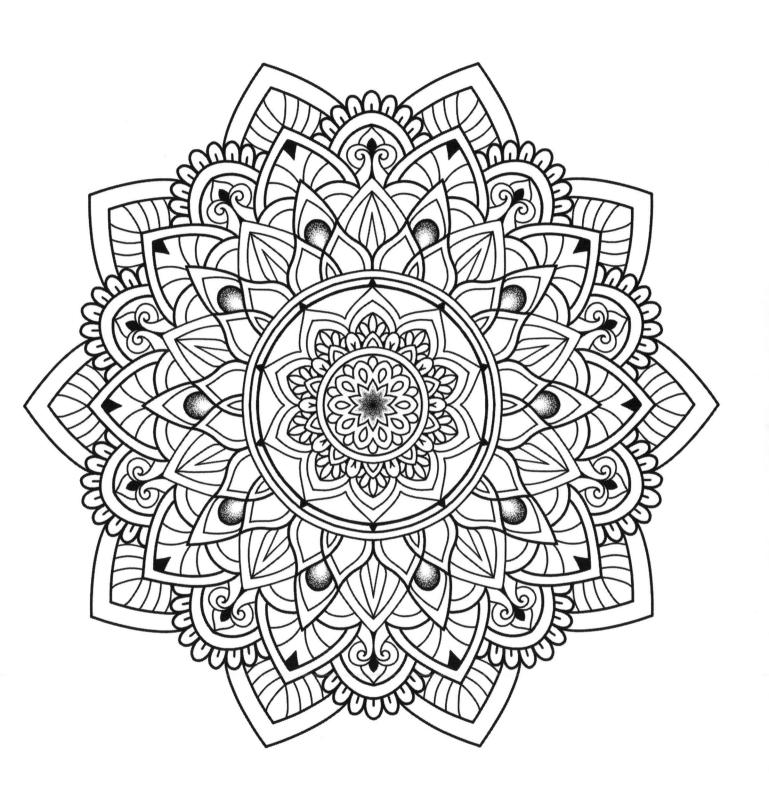

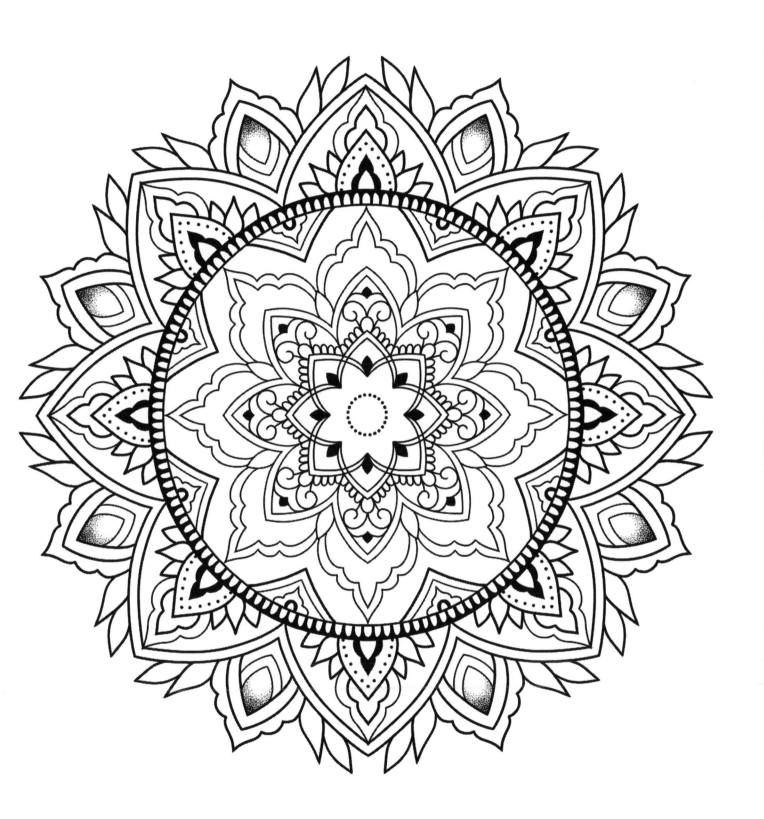

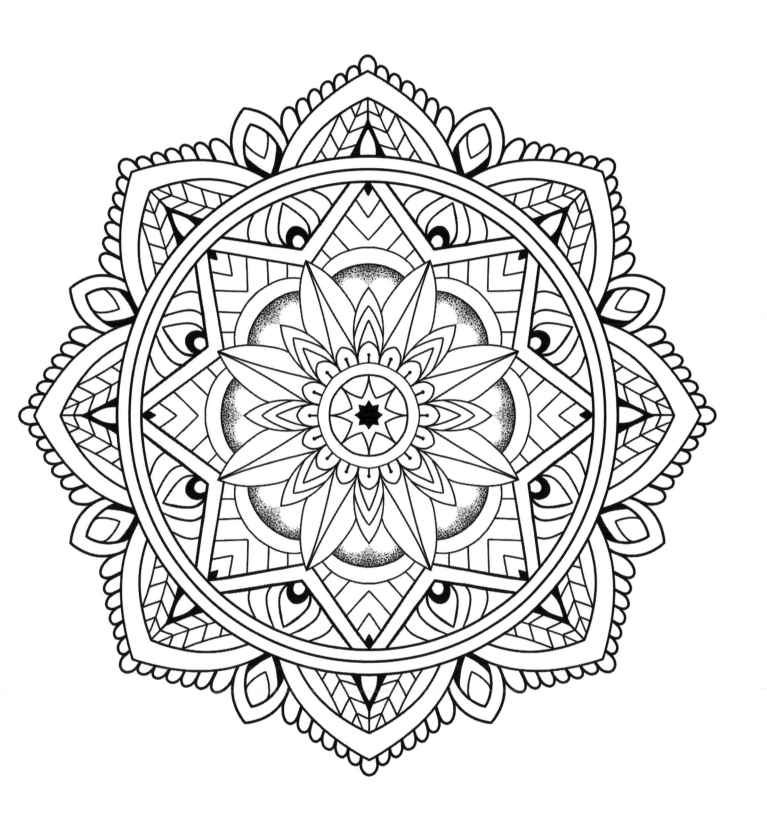

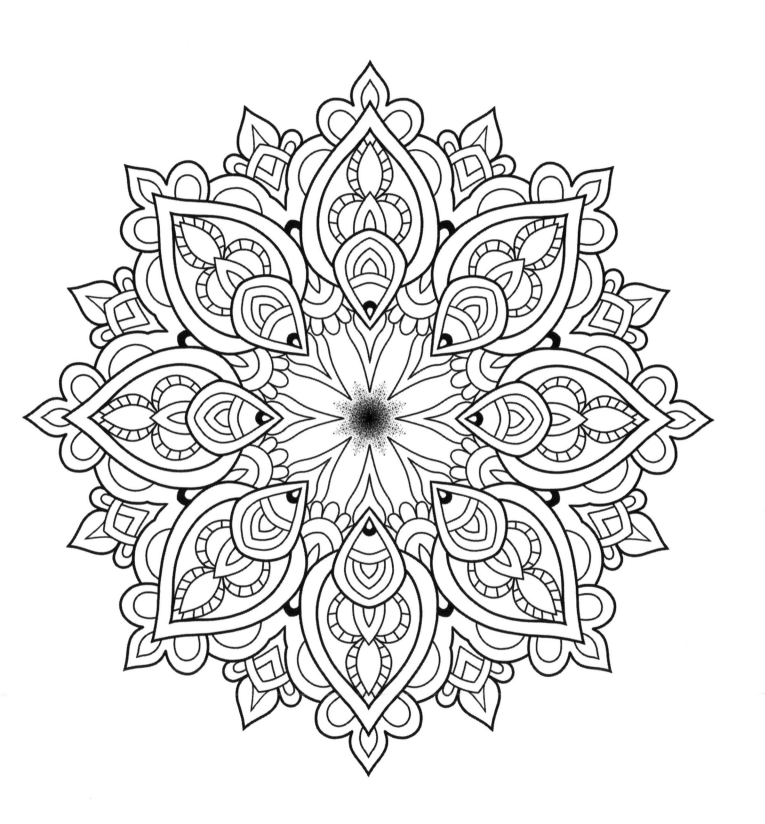

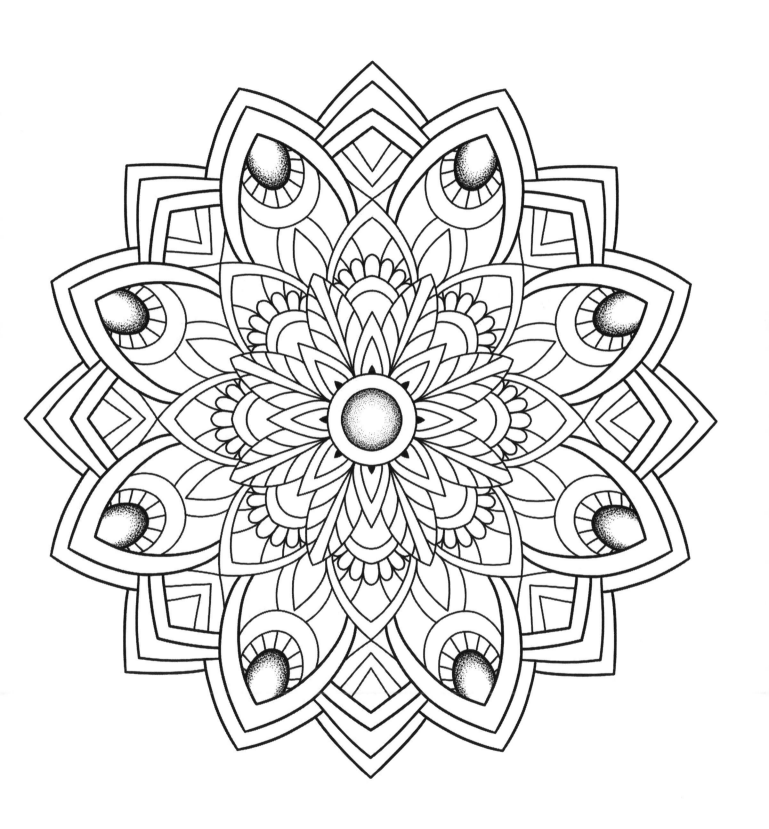

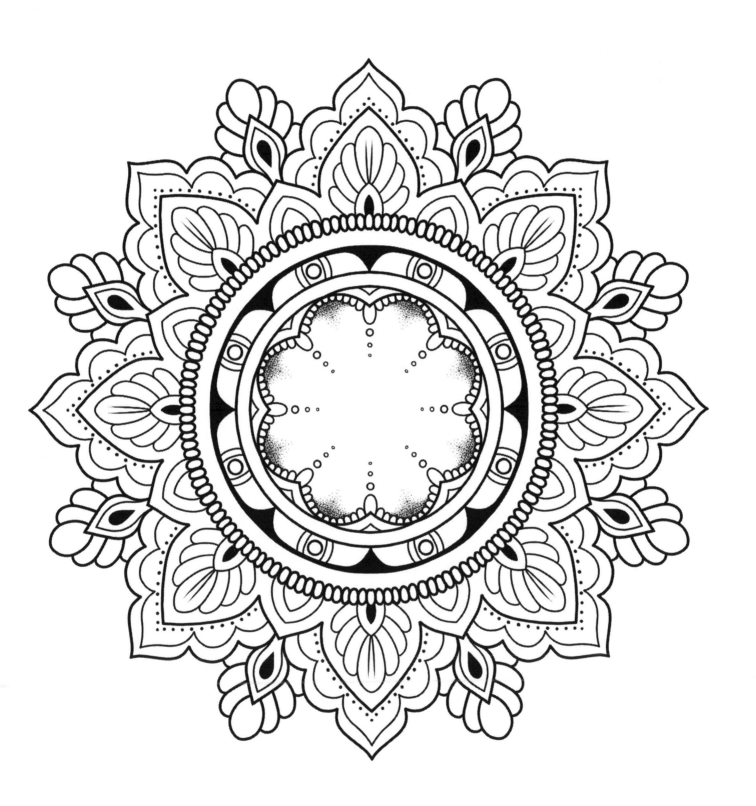

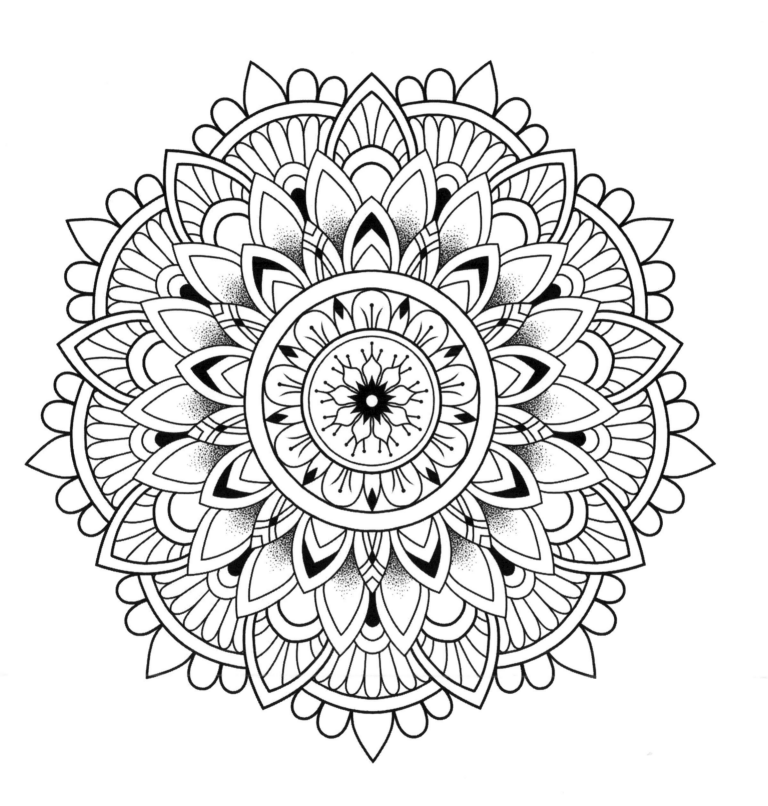

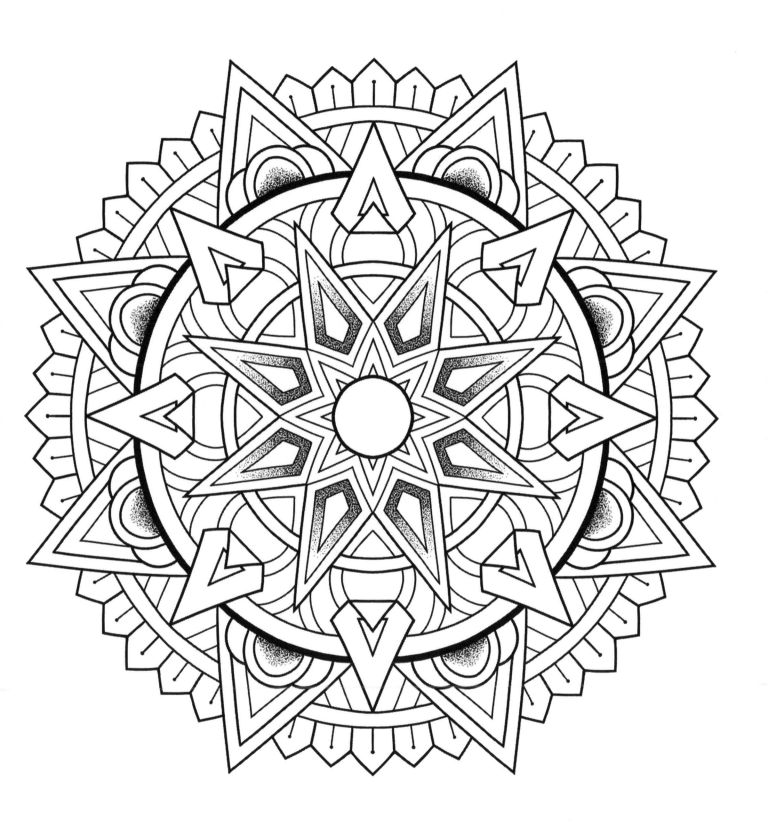

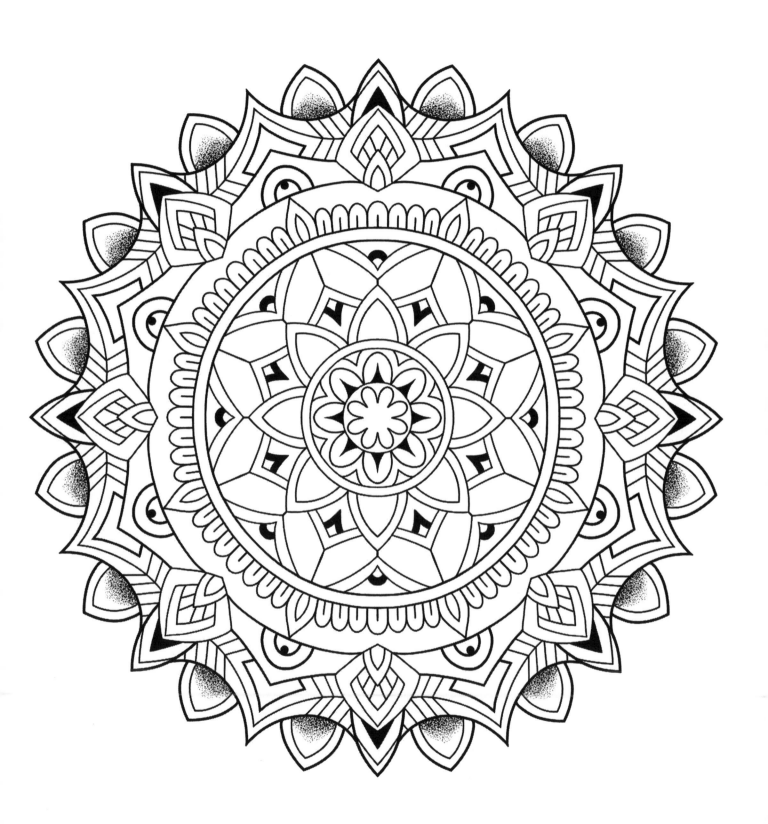

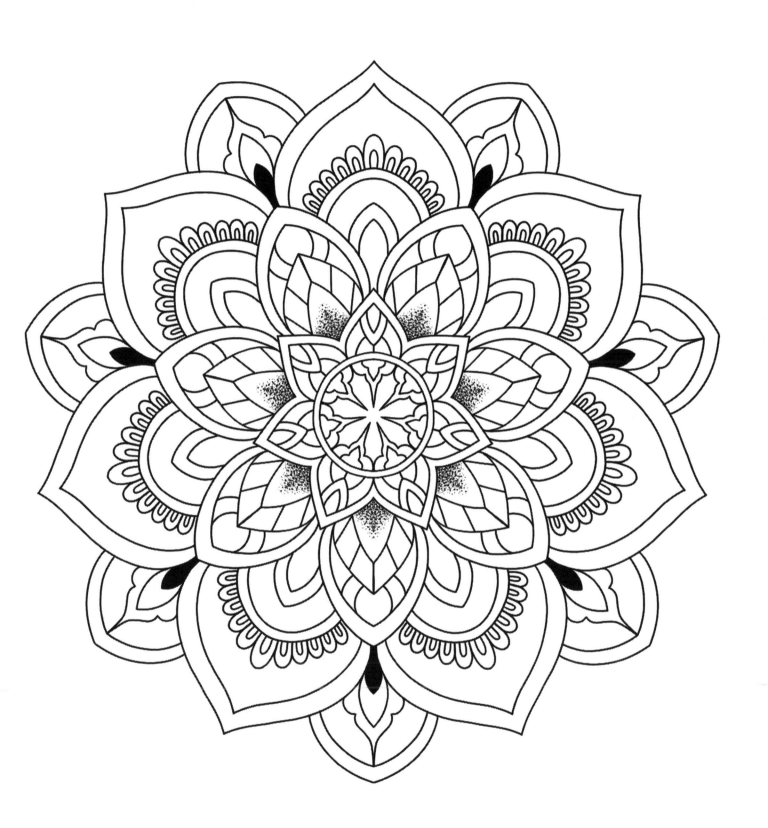

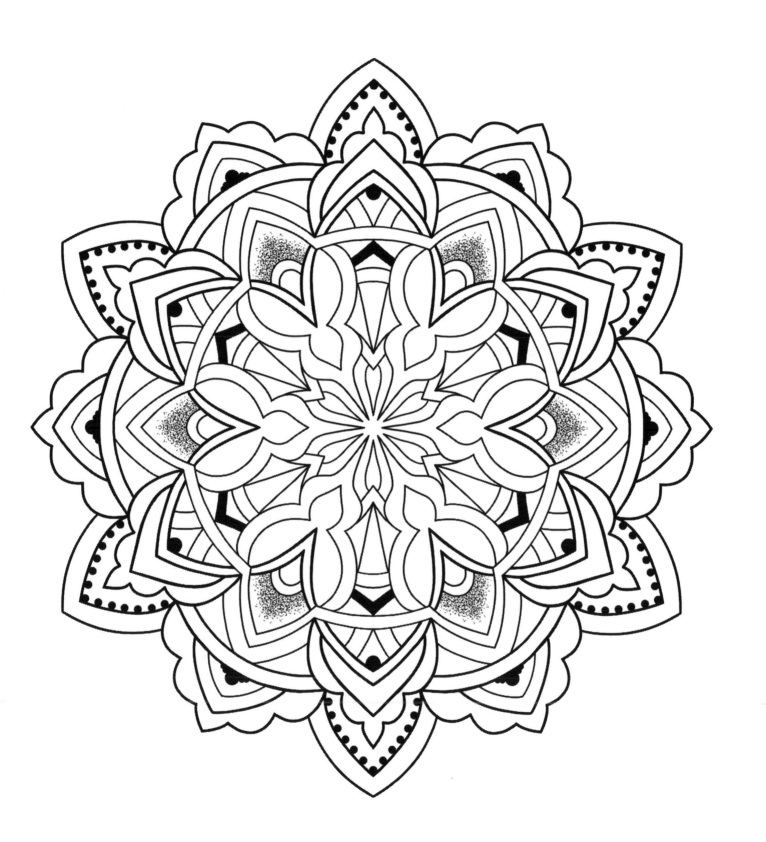

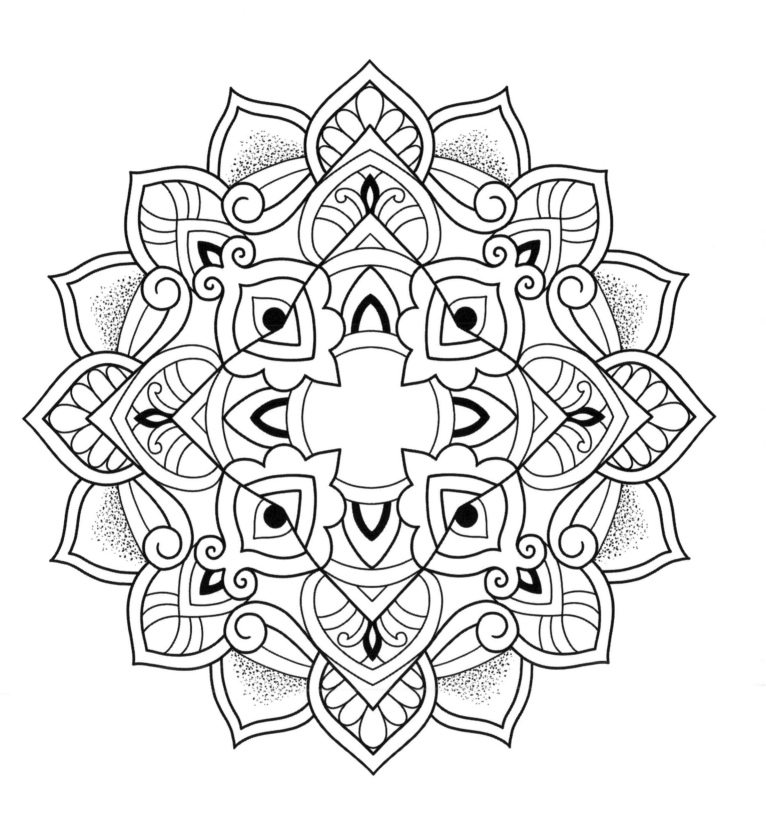

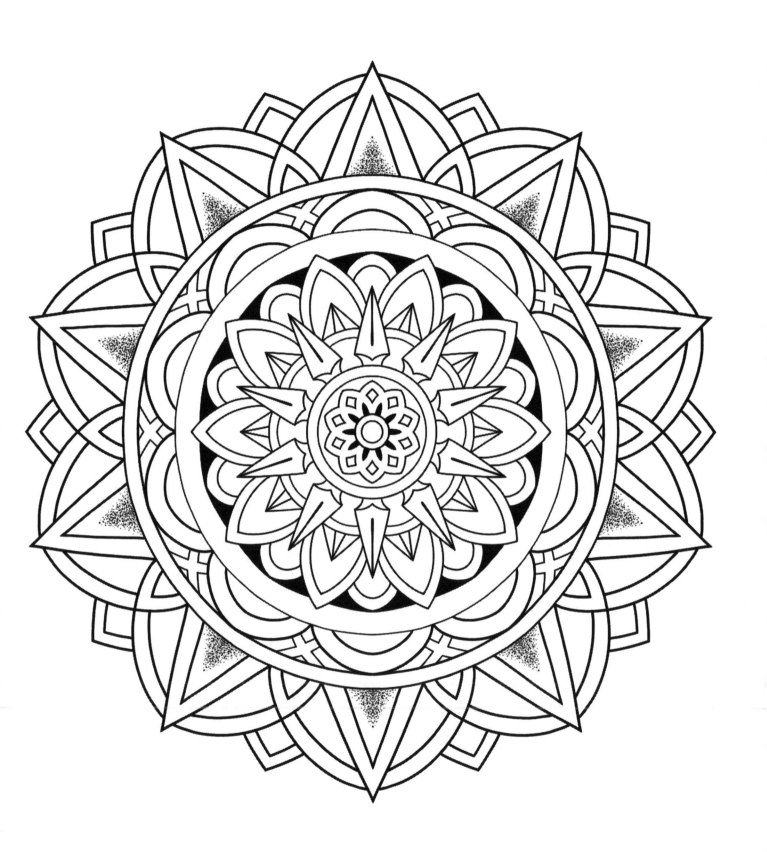

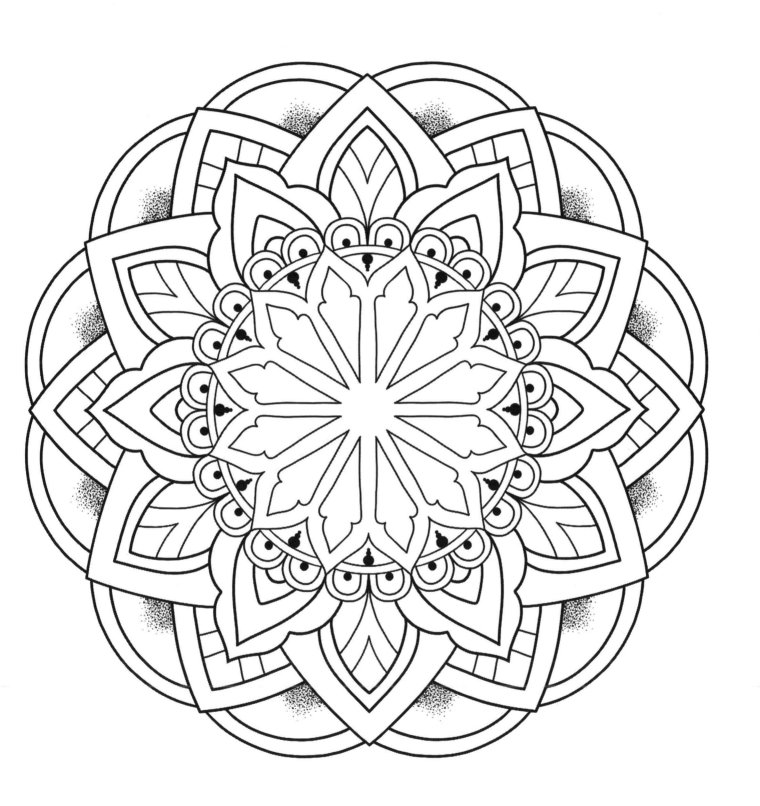

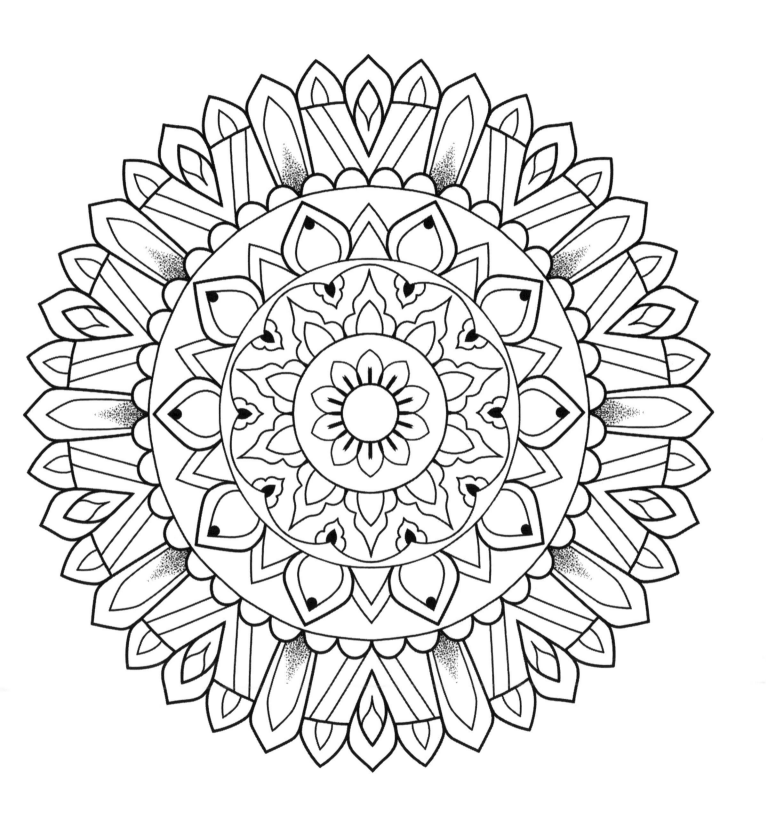

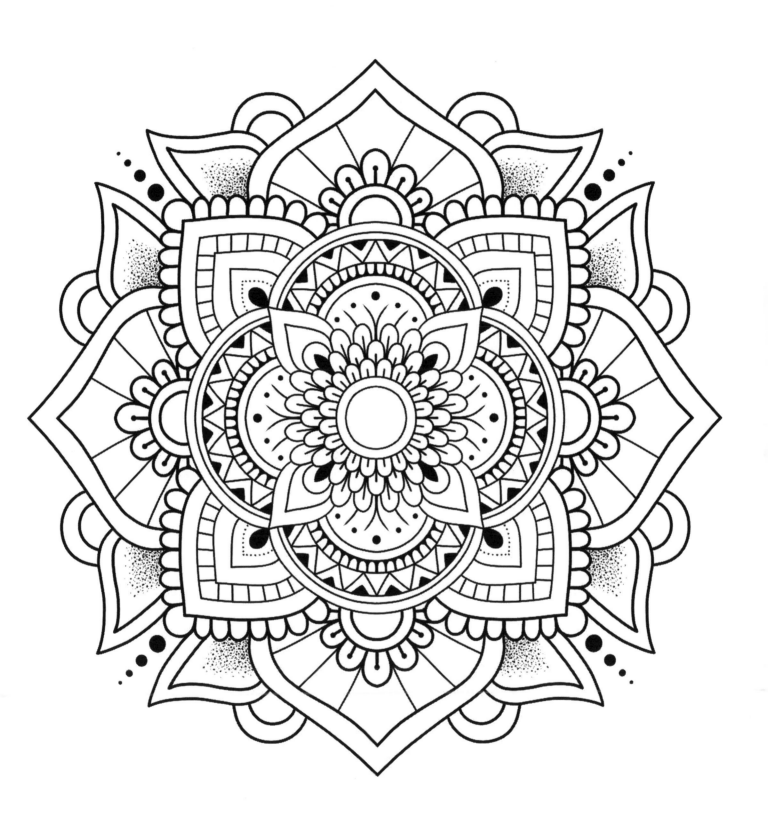

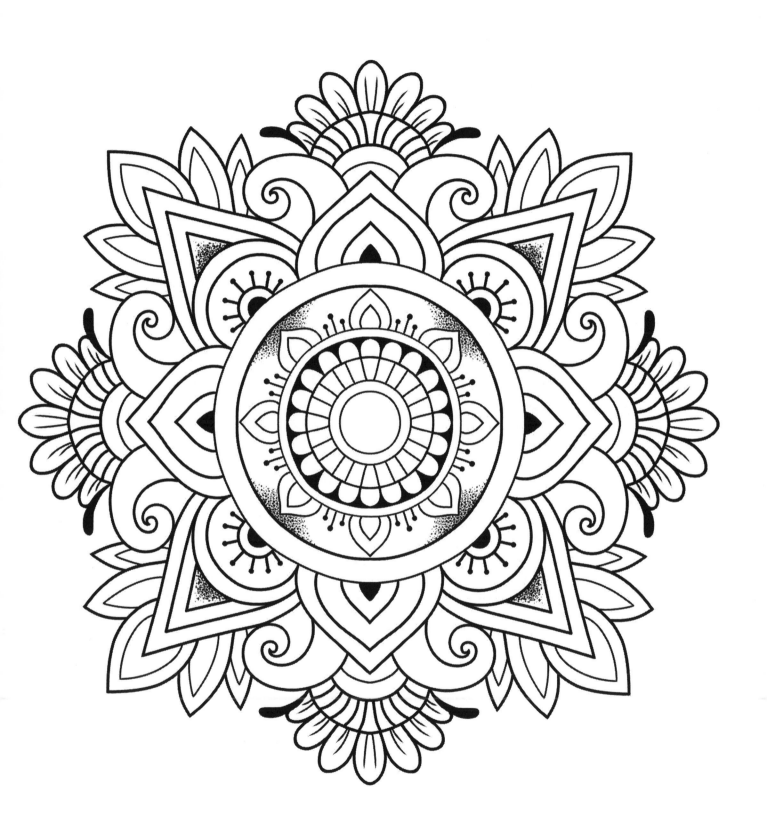

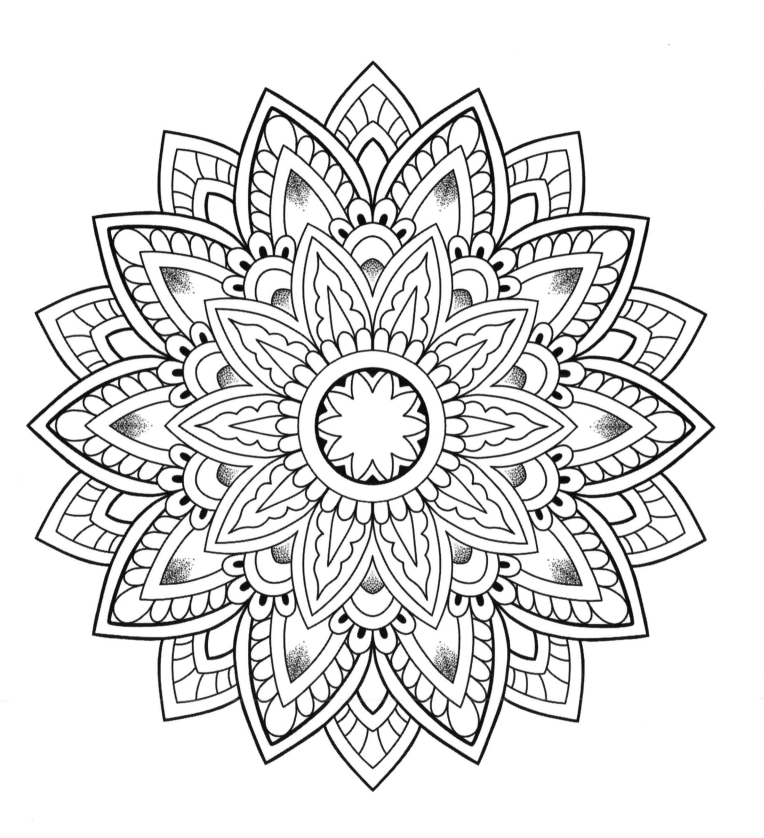

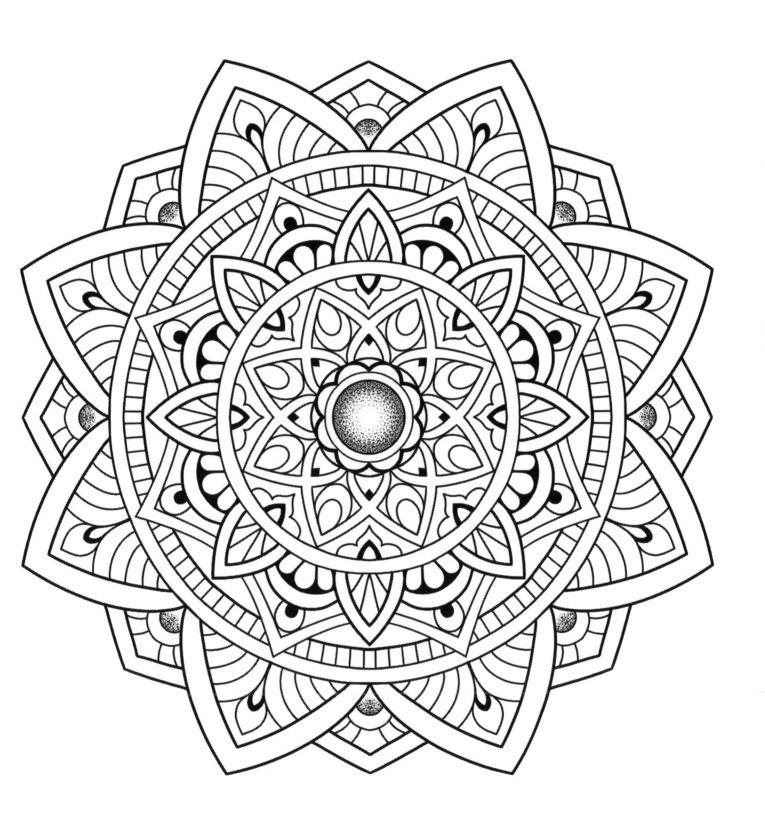

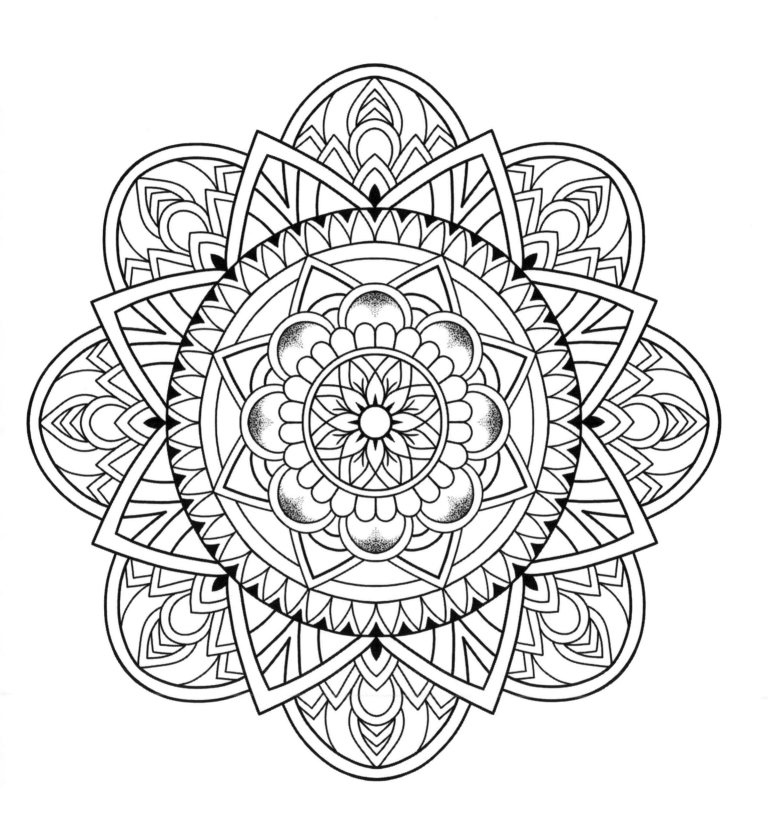

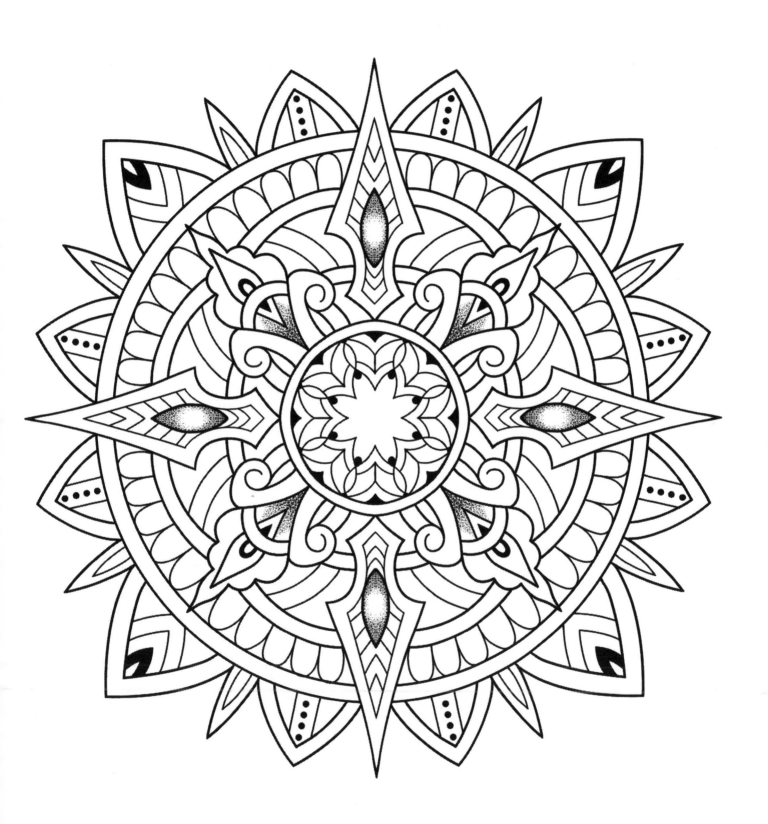

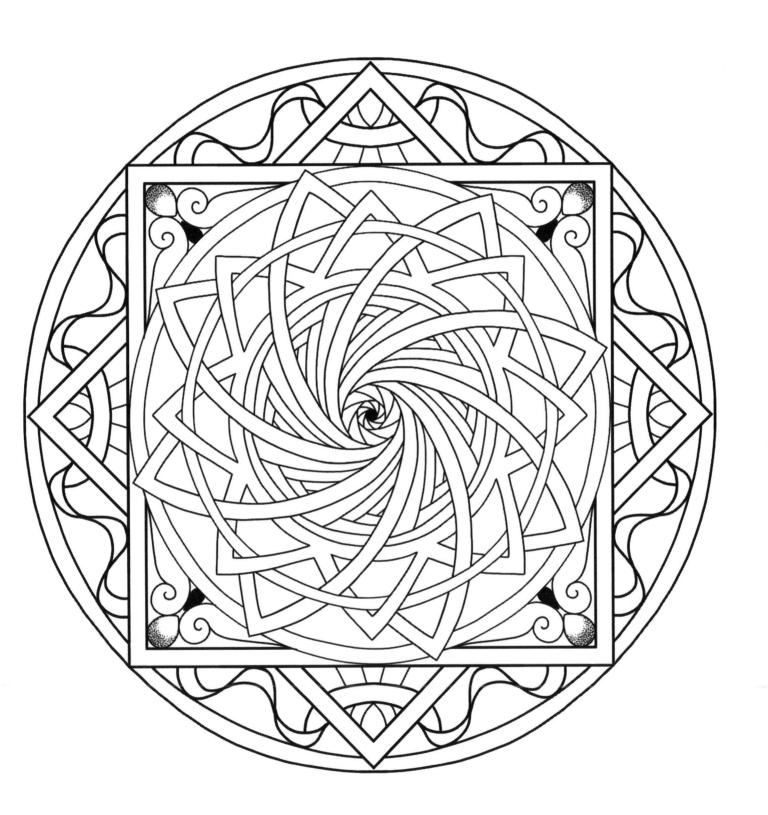

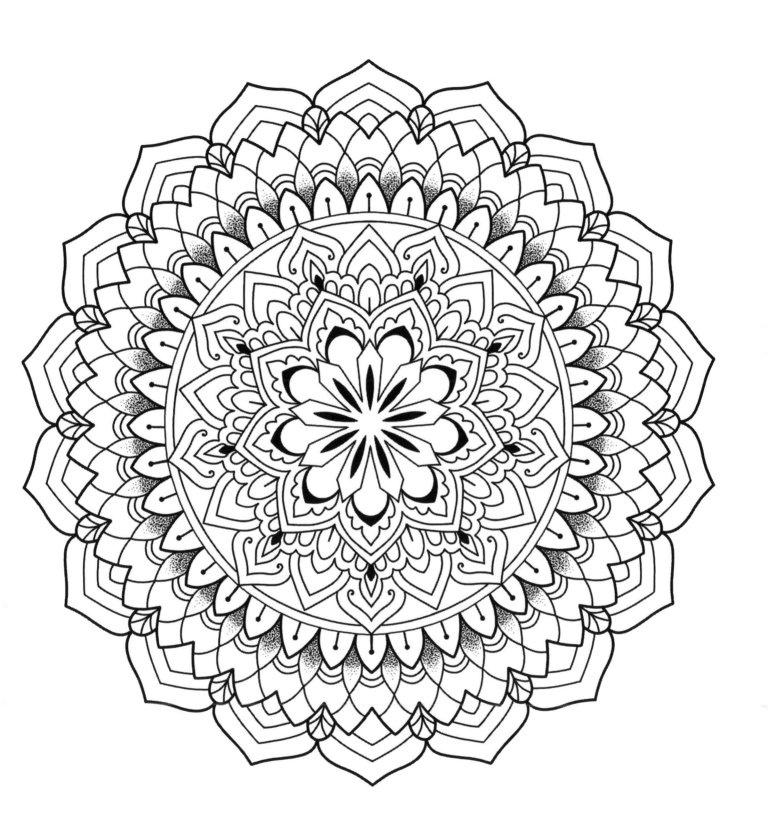

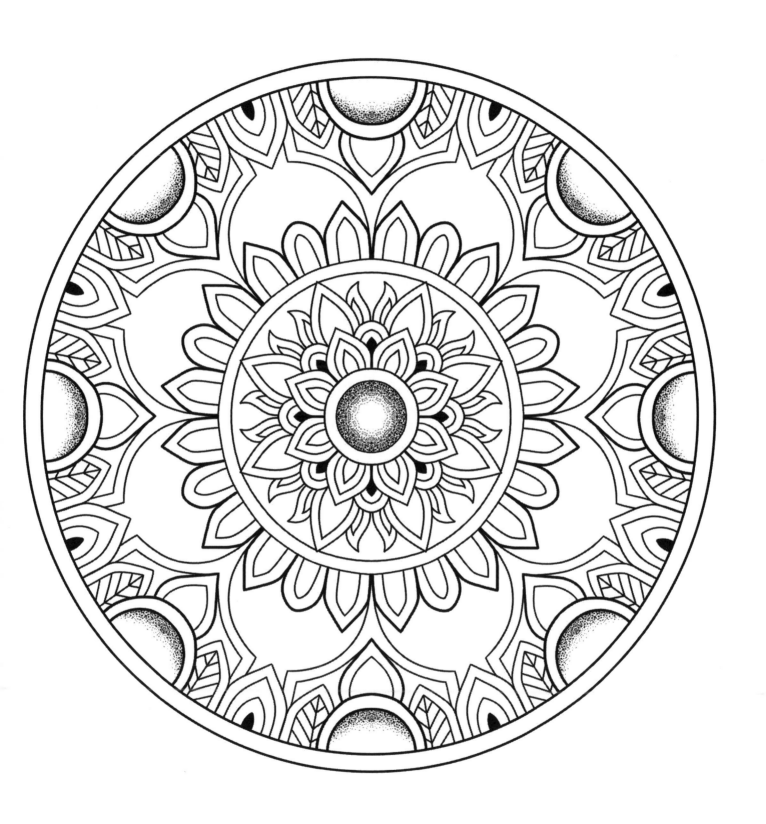

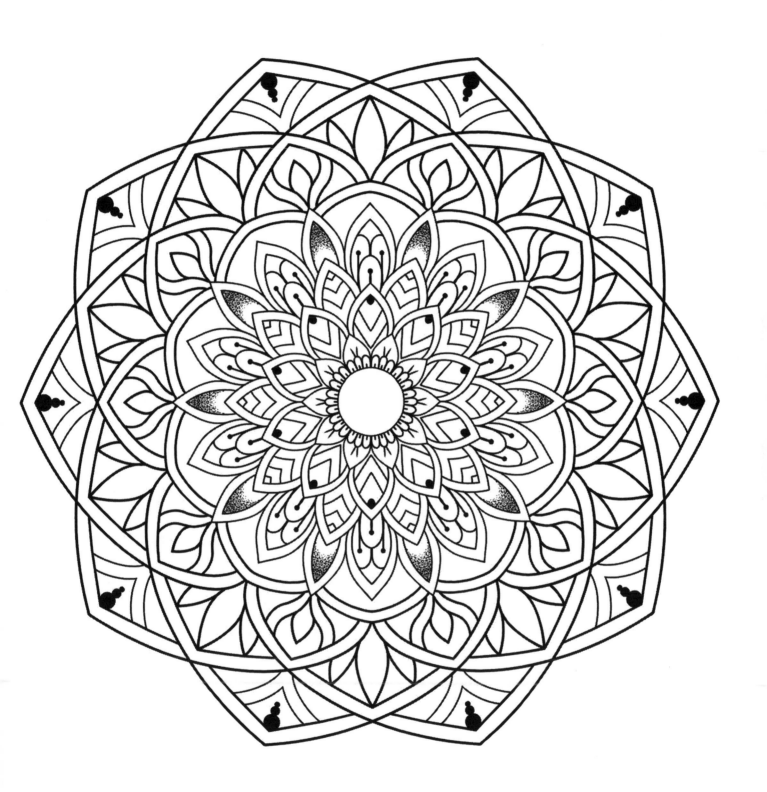

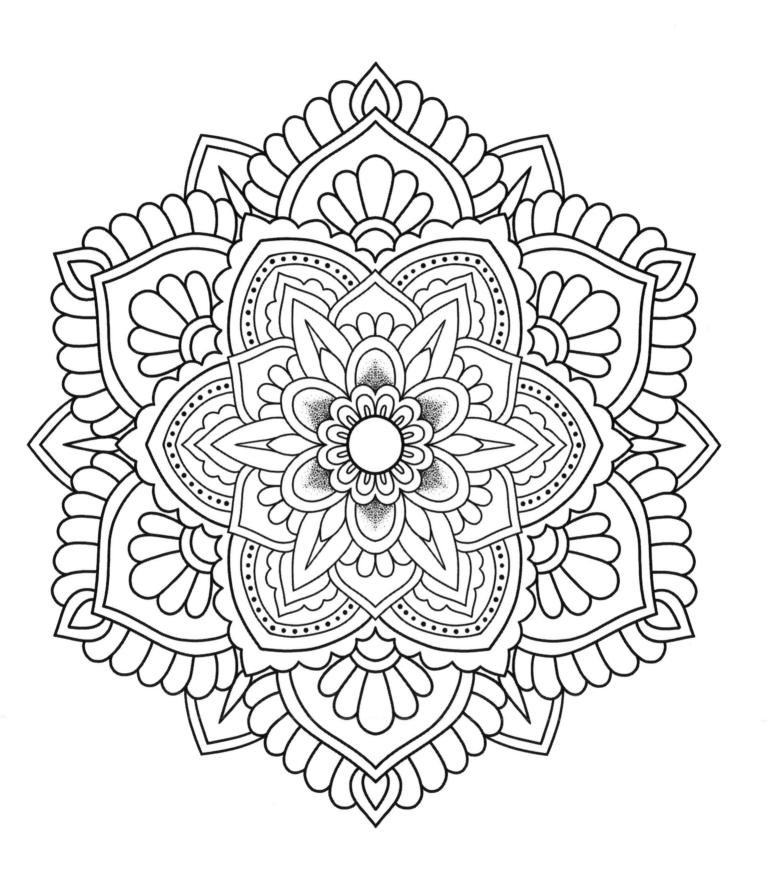

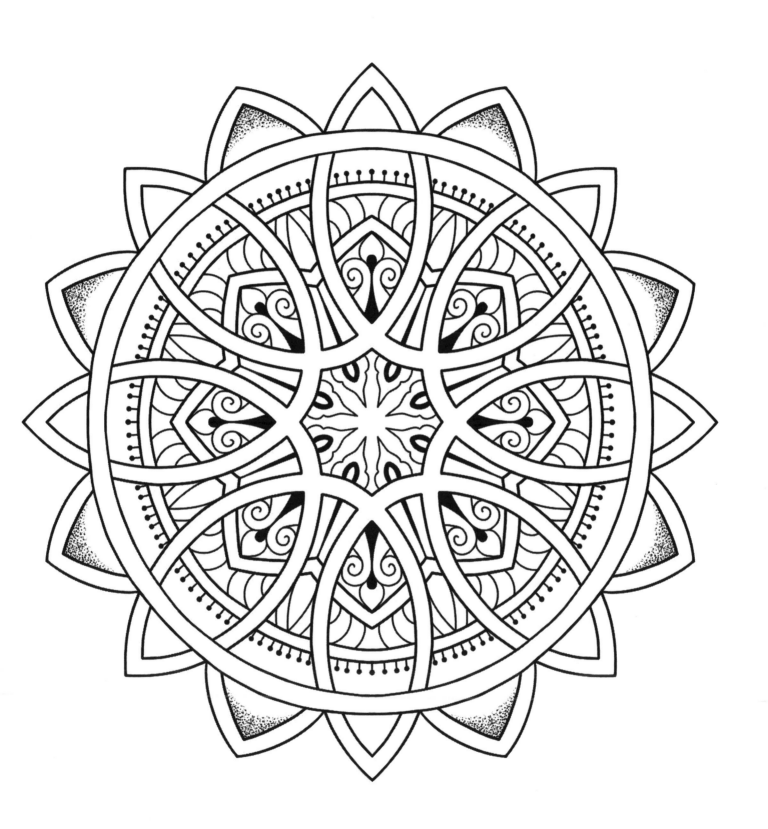

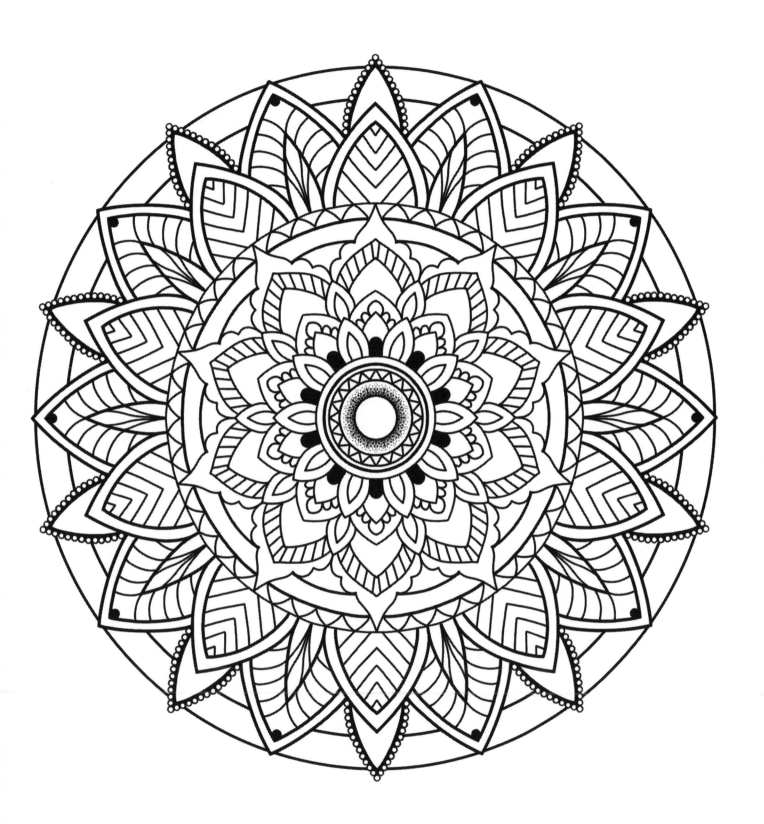

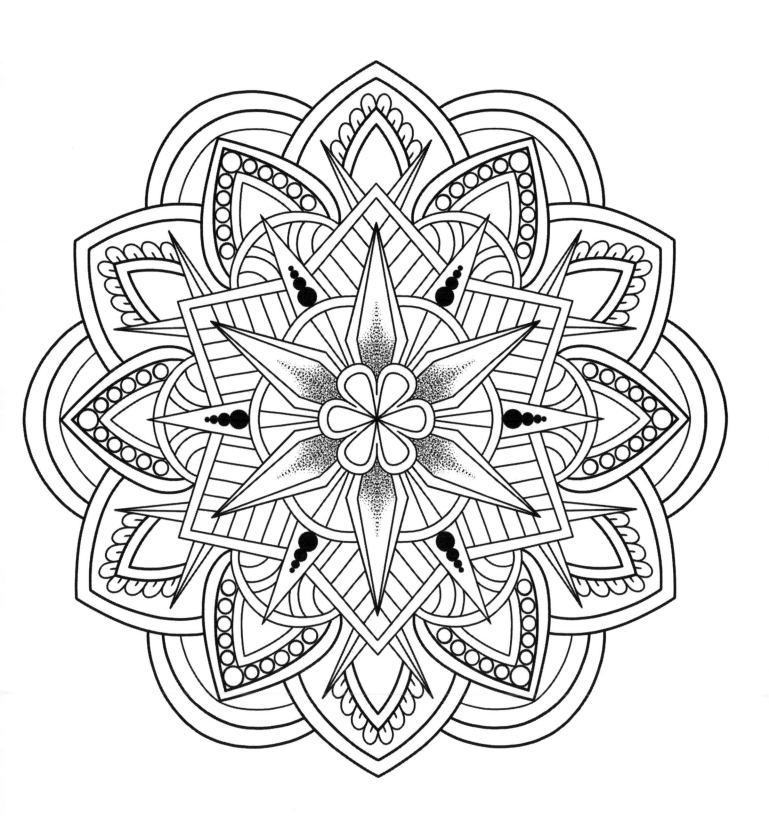

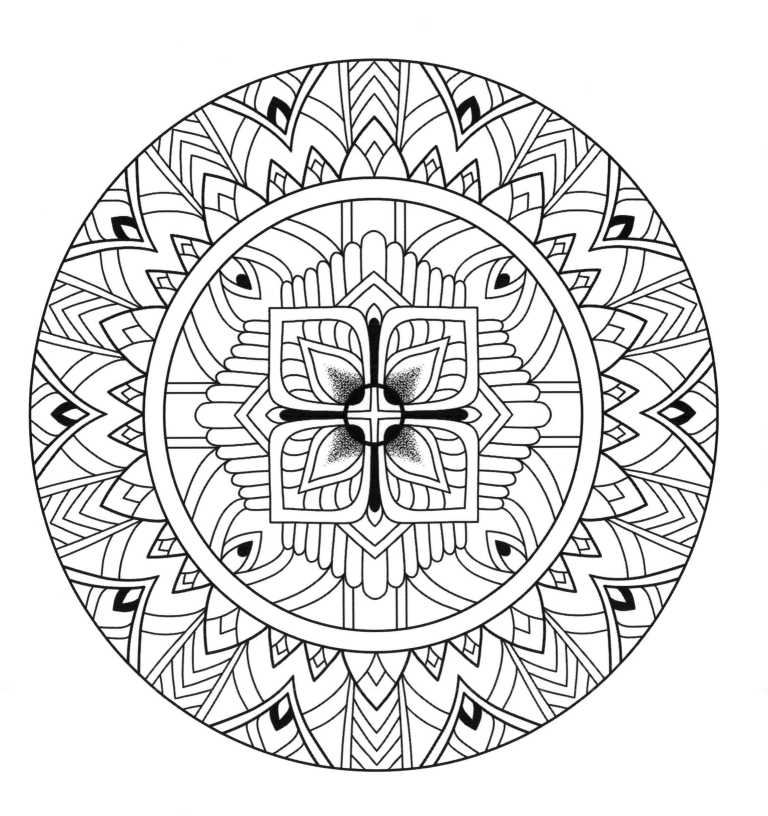

Made in the USA
Columbia, SC
09 September 2021